Fangs, Claws & Talons

Fangs, Claws & Talons

ANIMAL PREDATORS

CLARK BOOKS

A Division of Sterling Publishing Co., Inc.
New York / London

Author: Ada Spada
Editor: Veronika Alice Gunter
Illustrators: Filippo Cappellini and Maria Mantovani
Translator: Amy Gulick
Creative Director: Celia Naranjo
Designer: Robin Gregory
Art Director: Eleonora Barsotti
Art Production Assistant: Bradley Norris
Editorial Assistance: Rose McLarney

Spada, Ada.
  [Animali predatori. English]
  Fangs, claws & talons : animal predators / Ada Spada.
      p. cm.
  ISBN-13: 978-1-60059-150-1 (hardcover-plc : alk. paper)
  ISBN-10: 1-60059-150-7 (hardcover-plc : alk. paper)
  1. Predatory animals--Juvenile literature. I. Title.
  QL758.S63 2007
  591.5'3--dc22
                          2007009268

10 9 8 7 6 5 4 3 2 1

Published in 2007 by Lark Books, A Division of
Sterling Publishing Co., Inc.
387 Park Avenue South, New York, N.Y. 10016

Original title: Animali Predatori
by Ant's Books, Via Nazionale al Piemonte 40, 17100 Savona, Italy
Copyright © Renzo Barsotti 2005

English translation copyright © 2007 Lark Books

Distributed in Canada by Sterling Publishing,
c/o Canadian Manda Group, 165 Dufferin Street
Toronto, Ontario, Canada M6K 3H6

Distributed in the United Kingdom by GMC Distribution Services,
Castle Place, 166 High Street, Lewes, East Sussex, England BN7 1XU

Distributed in Australia by Capricorn Link (Australia) Pty Ltd.,
P.O. Box 704, Windsor, NSW 2756 Australia

If you have questions or comments about this book, please contact:
Lark Books
67 Broadway
Asheville, NC 28801
(828) 253-0467

Manufactured in China

ISBN 13: 978-1-60059-150-1
ISBN 10: 1-60059-150-7

For information about custom editions, special sales, premium and corporate purchases, please contact Sterling Special Sales Department at 800-805-5489 or specialsales@sterlingpub.com.

Contents

Predators and Prey

Every animal eats something—or someone! Predators are animals that hunt, kill, and eat other animals. The hunted animals are called prey. In this book you'll get up-close to tigers, bears, crocodiles, and more wild creatures as they catch their victims. You'll also see first-hand how skunks, hedgehogs, porcupine fish, and other prey escape becoming lunch.

An animal's looks and behaviors reveal what it eats—or what eats it. These characteristics give each animal its place in the food chain: the natural order of what eats what in the wild.

How Predators Succeed

When you see long fangs, razor-sharp claws, or talons on an animal, you're looking at a predator. A successful hunt means a predator will have the food necessary to grow, mate, and feed and raise its young.

Each species of predator has developed its own special set of traits and skills. For instance, the leopard has a spotted coat of fur. Its coloration helps in the hunt as much as its sharp fangs do. Those spots provide camouflage, helping the leopard blend in with the plants around it as it stalks antelopes. Without its spots, the leopard couldn't sneak up close enough to catch these fast animals, and it would go hungry.

Big mammals aren't the world's only hunters: many insects, amphibians, and reptiles are predators, too. What they hunt is often very small, but these animals have special traits and skills, too. Their survival depends on it.

How Prey Survive

Prey animals usually aren't the fiercest-looking animals in the wild. Most don't have the big teeth and massive, muscular bodies that some predators do. But in the life and death battle for survival, prey are far from helpless. They must stay alive to breed and raise the next generation of their species, so they adapt their skills and natural tools to their survival needs.

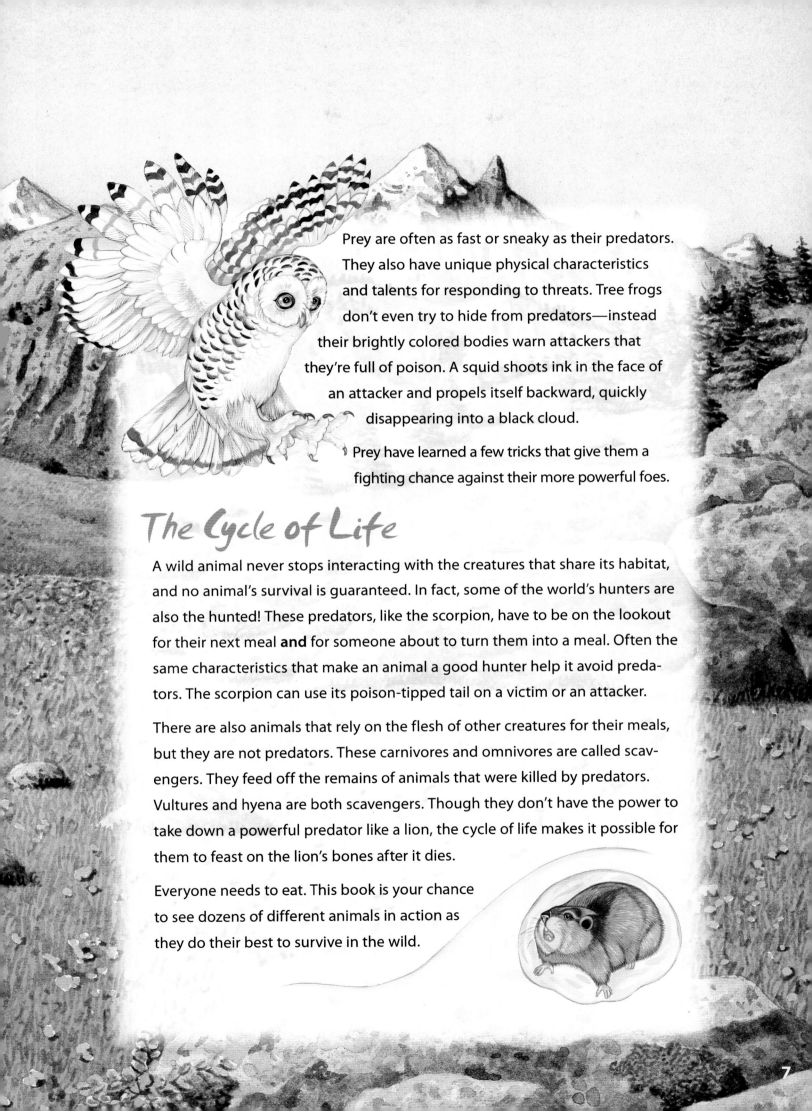

Prey are often as fast or sneaky as their predators. They also have unique physical characteristics and talents for responding to threats. Tree frogs don't even try to hide from predators—instead their brightly colored bodies warn attackers that they're full of poison. A squid shoots ink in the face of an attacker and propels itself backward, quickly disappearing into a black cloud.

Prey have learned a few tricks that give them a fighting chance against their more powerful foes.

The Cycle of Life

A wild animal never stops interacting with the creatures that share its habitat, and no animal's survival is guaranteed. In fact, some of the world's hunters are also the hunted! These predators, like the scorpion, have to be on the lookout for their next meal **and** for someone about to turn them into a meal. Often the same characteristics that make an animal a good hunter help it avoid predators. The scorpion can use its poison-tipped tail on a victim or an attacker.

There are also animals that rely on the flesh of other creatures for their meals, but they are not predators. These carnivores and omnivores are called scavengers. They feed off the remains of animals that were killed by predators. Vultures and hyena are both scavengers. Though they don't have the power to take down a powerful predator like a lion, the cycle of life makes it possible for them to feast on the lion's bones after it dies.

Everyone needs to eat. This book is your chance to see dozens of different animals in action as they do their best to survive in the wild.

Fast Animals

Moving with agility is an essential trait for many animals. Fast running, swimming, or flying is vital for hunters as well as for prey. Thousands of years of natural selection have made each predator more and more competitive and ready to move fast to capture prey.

The cheetah is a speed champion. It can reach running speeds up to 70 miles per hour. Given the enormous output of energy required, this large feline can maintain its incredible pace for only a few dozen seconds. If its prey is not captured within a few hundred meters, the cheetah must give up the chase, having exhausted its energy. (Meanwhile, gazelles and other prey can continue running away at top speed.) The peak speed is reached in just four seconds, thanks to the incredible acceleration allowed by the cheetah's powerful muscles. While running, the cheetah is able to maintain contact with the ground through its claws, which do not retract into the paws.

Peregrine Falcon

Speed, power, and hooked claws enable the peregrine falcon to capture birds, rodents, and fish. The bird dives at a rate of more than 200 miles per hour, slamming into its victim and stabbing it with its talons. Its sharp beak tears prey into bite-size pieces. These predators live on every continent except Antarctica and nest in any high spot, including desert cliffs and skyscrapers.

Common Swift

The common swift catches flying insects in mid-air, and it also drinks, bathes, mates, and sleeps while flying! These small birds soar and swoop by riding air currents. To hunt, they open their bills and create an air-funneling effect that sucks prey into their mouths.

The Sloth

Why run if you don't have to? The sloth is a small mammal of the South American rain forest—and the world's slowest animal. When it's on the move, it travels just six feet in a minute. By hiding in plain sight, unsuspecting prey, such as insects and lizards, walk right up to it, while predators walk right by.

In the Water

Animals that live in the world's lakes, seas, rivers, and oceans don't let water slow them down. Their bodies are tapered to glide through the water. The tuna fish is one of the fastest, whizzing by at 50 miles per hour. Different species of tuna pursue squid, shellfish, and other fish in seas all over the world. The penguin is the world's fastest bird—in the water. One species swims at a rate of up to 15 miles per hour. The penguin hustles to catch fish, krill, and squid in its sharp beak—and to escape seals, sharks, and other predators.

Ostrich

The ostrich can't fly, but it has learned to run as fast as other birds soar. Standing five to nine feet tall, this bird has long, strong legs that push it as fast as 45 miles per hour. Since the ostrich only hunts insects, its speed is most useful for making hasty escapes from predators. If that fails, the ostrich uses its legs to deliver powerful kicks and deep punctures from its large hooked claws.

Birds of Prey

An owl conducts its hunt in silence, moving its wings slowly and almost soundlessly as it flies low to the ground in forests and fields around the world. The owl has incredible hearing that allows it to listen for the movements of mice, raccoons, squirrels, voles, and other prey. It swoops talons-first, surprising prey and delivering fatal punctures. The owl can swallow small prey whole and regurgitate the fur and bones later. It carries larger prey back to the nest, tearing it into morsels with its narrow beak.

Predators that rely on knife-like talons and sharp, hooked beaks for killing and eating are called birds of prey, or raptors. Some birds of prey hunt at night, like the owl. Hawks, eagles, and other raptors hunt during the day. Each bird has specially developed traits that make it a formidable hunter in its habitat.

Nocturnal Eyes

A night that looks pitch black to you can seem bright as day to an owl. That's because an owl's eyes have many cells called rods that are able to pick up the faintest glints of light. The eyes are also large, so the owl has more opportunities to detect light—but they can't move in the eye sockets. To look around, the owl must move its head— nearly all the way around!

Secretary Bird

The African raptor called the secretary or Sagittarius bird likes to pounce on and grab its prey with its razor-sharp talons. Then it zooms up into the sky with a few flaps of its seven-foot wide wings and drops the prey. It recovers the crushed snake, lizard, or mouse from the ground and carries the meal back to its nest to eat.

Snowy Owl

The snowy owl doesn't need to fly in search of a meal. The pattern of colors on its feathers allows this raptor to blend in with its Arctic habitat, so it can perch and wait for prey to make a sound. The snowy owl's favorite food is the lemming, a small rodent that nests under snow. The owl can hear a lemming inside its nest and plunge toward the victim, bursting through the snow to make the kill.

Eagle

Of all the predators that hunt in daylight, the golden eagle may have the best sight. It soars above mountainous areas throughout the Northern Hemisphere, flying in circles that widen with each pass. In an instant, it can notice movement thousands of feet below and make a nosedive at the target. If it's a bird or small animal, the eagle slams its powerful rear talon into the victim and then grasps the prey with its other hooked claws. The eagle may eat its catch on the spot or tote it back to its nest.

Talons

A talon is the perfect tool for getting an inescapable hold on prey.

Birds of prey rely on strong foot muscles to power their sharp talons—and for many other actions. They clutch onto perches for stability and stretch their toes far apart to get a secure grip on prey.

Curved Beaks

Raptors don't need teeth to rip apart the bodies of their prey. They're equipped with horn-like mouthparts called beaks that stick out from their heads. Like talons, beaks are hooked or curved down to a sharp point. Curved beaks rip through even the toughest flesh as if it were paper.

Forest Predators

The world's forests are home to a wide variety of predators and their prey. In colder climates, it's hard to find food—especially enough food for large predators that need to eat a lot. Bears will eat all they can during the summer and then hibernate during the winter to save energy. Pine martens, wolves, foxes, and wolverines have also developed tools and skills that help them succeed in their year-round hunt for prey.

As summer ends, fish called salmon begin swimming upstream to breed in the rivers of North America. Grizzly bears and Kodiak bears like to eat salmon and know which streams the fish return to each year. These bears can weigh more than 1,300 pounds and sprint up to 30 miles per hour. To hunt fish, the bear waits in parts of the stream where the prey must jump into the air on their journey. With a quick swipe of one massive, clawed paw or a chomp of its huge mouth, the bear catches its victim. These bears make salmon the last meal of the year before choosing a cave for a long winter's nap.

Wolf

The wolf constantly searches for prey and can travel for miles on its long legs without tiring. Its nose and the smell glands along its jaws guide the wolf, allowing it to pick up the scent of bison, musk oxen, moose, elk, and reindeer more than a mile away. The wolf hunts large prey in packs, but a lone wolf can easily take down small animals, such as rabbits.

Pine Marten

The pine marten is an unshakable predator that will run, climb, jump, and swim in pursuit of its prey. At dawn and dusk, it chases down mice on the forest floor, scrambles up tree trunks after squirrels, leaps from limb to limb to ambush birds in their nests, and dives after fish in the streams of its pine-forest habitat.

Fox

The fox is a cunning small canine that has adapted to thrive everywhere from forests to human neighborhoods. Foxes are omnivores that eat everything from fresh fruit and small animals to discarded human food. The fox hunts alone at night, targeting mice, rabbits, birds, and voles with its keen senses of smell and hearing. The fox sneaks up on its padded feet, pounces to knock the victim down, and delivers just one deadly bite with its short, powerful jaws and teeth.

Wolf Packs

Wolves lead a social life, forming small packs led by a dominant female and male pair. Working as a pack allows wolves to use hunting strategies that improve their chances of capturing large prey that can provide a meal for all the wolves. Before launching an attack, a pack chooses a young or weak victim that should be easy to kill. The wolves circle the victim and injure it with bites to its rump and sides. To make the kill, a wolf grabs the animal's throat—steering clear of horns, hoofs, and other dangerous parts a deer or other prey may use to defend itself.

Wolverine

The wolverine is known for using its razor-sharp claws and teeth to capture and kill prey—and to battle a bear over territory or a meal. The largest member of the weasel family, it can weigh up to 70 pounds. It takes down deer twice its size and eats it in one meal. This behavior earned the wolverine the nickname "the glutton."

Underwater Predators

Just like predators on land, some hunters of the sea use a high-speed chase to make the kill, while others hide and ambush their prey. But unlike wolves, bears, and many other land-dwelling hunters, most underwater predators are also prey. Only the largest sharks and the fiercest whales can hunt without concern for what might be hunting them!

More than 250 species of sharks roam the Earth's waters. The most ferocious species are great white sharks and tiger sharks. They hunt every type of fish and sea creature. Seals are a favorite snack of the great white shark. Losing a tooth is never a problem for these predators—they have multiple rows of teeth, and each tooth can grow back if lost. Tiger sharks hunt in packs. They swim in circles and crisscrossing patterns to trap their prey in a feeding frenzy that leaves the water bright with the blood of their victims.

Killer Whale

The largest predator in the sea isn't a fish—it's the killer whale, a mammal that can grow more than 30 feet in length and weigh up to 7 tons. (That's the same size as three small cars or one big truck!) Killer whales, also called orcas, rely on their massive jaws and explosive speed to hunt under water and also right up to the edges of ice and dry land. Seals are a favorite snack for this huge hunter. Orcas live in groups and often attack seals, fish, and other whales as a pack.

Sea Anemone

The sea anemone looks like a flower growing on the sea floor near ocean coasts all over the world. Don't be fooled! This predator attracts fish in search of an easy meal and waits for prey to brush against one of its hair-thin tentacles. The sea anemone clutches its victim and stings it with a paralyzing poison. It finishes off the helpless animal by thrusting it into its hidden mouth.

Common Angler

A hungry fish sees a delicious, wiggling worm in its cold, deep-sea habitat. It swims closer to investigate. But before it can take a bite, a mouth much larger than its own opens out of the ocean floor—and the fish is swallowed whole! A common angler has lured its prey using a fin dangling from its head.

Octopus

The octopus has excellent vision and can change color to blend into its surroundings in the temperate oceans of the world. This makes it easy to stalk crustaceans and fish on its nighttime hunting raids. Taking the victim by surprise, the octopus grasps the prey with one suction-cup covered arm. It shoves the trapped animal into a beak-like mouth hidden on the underside of its body. The octopus's powerful mouth easily rips open crustacean shells to reveal the soft flesh inside.

Starfish

The starfish may look like a harmless, lumpy creature, but this predator has the tools and strength to eat any type of hard-shelled sea animal. It wraps its suction-cup-covered arms on either side of a mollusk and pulls to pry open the shell. Then it sticks its stomach out through its mouth, wraps the stomach around the soft body of the prey, and swallows it all back inside!

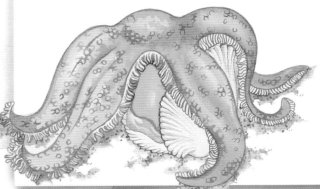

Pike

Pike are sometimes called freshwater sharks because they rule the cold, slow-moving rivers and still lakes of the world. With their sharp teeth, long jaws, and aggressive behavior, no predators hunt these large fish. Pike eat fish of all sizes, plus frogs and crayfish. They'll even leap of out their hiding places among riverbed grasses to catch birds!

Mouths Made for Hunting

Every predator develops unique natural tools and behaviors to be an effective hunter. For some animals, the mouth is an essential tool for capturing prey. Whether the predator's mouth is small with tiny teeth, large and fanged, or oddly shaped and toothless, it's deadly for the prey it hunts.

Crocodiles creep through saltwater rivers, oceans, and lakes with only their ears, eyes, and nostrils poking above the water's surface. Their stealth hides their enormous size, explosive attack speed, and deadly jaws and teeth. When prey is within reach, a crocodile shoots its 20-foot-long body forward with its massive mouth open wide. The prey is trapped between the teeth of its clenched jaws, dragged under water, and held until it drowns.

The crocodile hunts everything from birds to buffalo, often ambushing animals that come to the water to drink. It lives in the tropical regions of the world. Though the crocodile spends time both in the water and basking on land, it does most of its hunting in the water.

Piranha

The piranha has a relatively small mouth filled with tiny, jagged-edged teeth. This freshwater fish's aggressiveness makes it lethal to any creature it finds in the water. The piranha attacks by tearing away shreds of flesh, making the victim bleed so that other piranha taste the blood and rush to join the attack. In the feeding frenzy that follows, the fish can devour a large mammal within a few minutes, leaving only a skeleton.

Pelican

When flying or diving, the pelican has a long, narrow beak. The shape allows it to make fast, accurate dives aimed at underwater prey. Then the pelican opens its lower beak and extends a large skin pouch—scooping up dozens of small fish and gallons of water. The pelican lifts its head above water, spits out the water, and swallows the fish whole.

Felines

Carnivorous cats have short, strong jawbones and upper and lower fangs, all set in a heavy skull. Tigers and lions can get an inescapable, crushing grip on their prey and inflict a fatal bite. Their skulls can weigh more than six pounds, while a human skull weighs only two pounds.

A feline aims to sink its fangs deep into the neck of a victim, to kill the prey instantly. A cat's smaller front teeth are especially good at tearing away fur and flesh so it can access nutritious muscle tissue and internal organs. Its other teeth are adapted for chewing.

Alligator

The alligator lives in fresh water and in swampy areas of the United States and China where it hunts small mammals, fish, and crustaceans. The reptile's wide head and long jawbones make for a mouth that's perfect for capturing prey whole. Its grip offers no chance of escape. The alligator ambushes prey it finds drinking at the water's edge and snatches water-dwelling victims from murky riverbeds.

Cats

Cats all over the world share behaviors and traits that make them superb predators. But each feline species is also unique. A tiger has stripes from head to tail for camouflage. This coloration divides its body into small sections—which is a big help with hiding if you're a 10-foot long, 500-pound cat. An ocelot has small dark or bright-ringed spots atop a lighter-colored fur coat. Its colors vary, depending on whether the cat lives in the deserts of Central America or the forests of South America.

The tiger has a distinctive reddish-orange coat with black stripes. It's the world's largest and most powerful cat. The largest tigers live the furthest north: Siberian tigers can weigh more than 700 pounds, while Indonesian tigers weigh only about 200 pounds.

The tiger is native to hot tropical jungles and cold alpine forests in Asia. This feline hunts everything from the rhinoceros and the gazelle to the mountain hare. The tiger will often make long trips following the tracks of large prey, stalking the victim for days before chasing it down.

How Cats Attack

Every feline—from the lion to the housecat—attacks by moving in a forward jump called a pounce. The cat propels itself off the ground or from a tree with its powerful hind legs. It uses its tail for balance, swinging it from side to side as needed. If the cat makes a good pounce, it lands on the prey's back and knocks the animal to the ground. This leaves the victim's neck clear for a single lethal bite.

Ocelot

Leopard

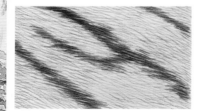

Tiger

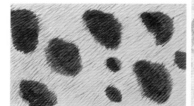

Cheetah

In the Water

Most cats would rather not get wet, but some felines use waterways for hunting grounds and a place to relax. The jaguar hunts frogs and fish in the Amazon River. Some species of tiger and the ocelot swim to cool off—and they sometimes play in water.

Spotted Coats

Spotted coats provide camouflage for felines on the hunt, making it hard for prey to recognize the body of its predator. You can tell cat species apart by looking at the shapes and colors of their spots. Each kind of cat has spots that match the colors of the plants in its habitat, making it easy for the feline to hide behind tall grasses, short shrubs, or even in trees.

Small Felines

Most of the world's feline species are small cats that capture and kill thousands of small mammals, fish, birds, and reptiles each year. One of these cats is the ocelot, a predator that's just a few pounds heavier and a few inches taller than a housecat. It must hunt more often than its larger relatives because each meal is smaller.

Claws

All cats take special care to exercise their feet and sharpen their claws so they're always ready to attack and rip flesh. Wild cats scratch on hard, destructible surfaces like wood to sharpen their claws. Most felines keep their claws retracted—pulled inside their toes—and protected when they aren't attacking, eating, or sharpening.

Hiding Prey

It's not easy to get enough to eat, even for big cats. Once they catch their prey, cats have to guard it from other animals that are ready to snatch it away. A pack of hyenas, for instance, will often attack a leopard to take its food because the hyenas know the cat may not have the energy to battle them all. Big cats solve this problem by dragging their meal to a high tree branch. The hyenas can't reach the food, and the cat can rest and eat.

Many Ways to Hunt

Some predators launch silent attacks that leave no chance for their prey to flee or fight. Though they may also possess traits like speed, strength, or camouflage, these hunters rely on their intricate webs, fast-acting poisons, and lightening-fast mouths and tongues for success.

The algae-colored archerfish has a lethal spit—but it doesn't use poison. This swamp-dweller blends in with the mangrove tree roots of its tropical habitat in Asia and India. Its coloration makes the fish invisible to small insects perched on leaves hanging over the water. The archerfish selects a victim and sips water into its mouth—only to blast the water at the prey in a powerful stream. The predator's spit flies up to four feet and strikes with deadly accuracy. The archerfish whizzes to the spot where the prey falls into the fish's open mouth.

Snake

Most snakes capture prey by wrapping their bodies around the victim. A snake will swallow prey while it's still alive and struggling, or wait and squeeze its victim until it suffocates. A few species of snakes have a secret weapon—venom. They strike prey with fangs, injecting poison through grooves or cavities in the fangs. The poison attacks the prey's nervous system, paralyzing it—or causing immediate death.

Spider

A spider weaves its web from silky, sticky thread it makes in its body. The threads are almost invisible but extremely strong—the golden orb spider captures birds in its three-foot wide webs! After weaving a web, the spider rests in the center, hidden in plain sight thanks to its camouflaging colors. When a flying animal touches the web it becomes stuck.

Chameleon

The chameleon is one of the few animals in the world that changes colors. And it's the only animal that has a tongue that can stretch to twice the length of its body! The reptile combines these traits with a super-quick flicking action and a sticky tongue tip to capture small insects that might escape other predators. The chameleon waits for prey on a branch in its forest habitat in Africa, Asia, India, and Europe. As the light and temperature change, so does the chameleon's skin, making it hard to see. When a victim is in range, the chameleon launches its tongue, striking and securing the prey— and then yanking the prey into its mouth faster than you can blink!

Bat

The bat is an acrobatic hunter that locates prey with its ears and then flips and turns through the air to silently fly in for the kill. The mammal lives in all but the coldest habitats of the world. Though they can see and smell well, most bat species hunt at night using their sense of hearing. The bat emits high-frequency sounds—sounds that even dogs cannot detect—and waits for the sounds to ricochet off of the insects it hunts. It hears the subtle echoes and flies to the prey, spinning sideways and upside down to avoid creating air currents that might warn the victim of its approach.

Praying Mantis

The praying mantis gets its name from how it folds its front legs under its head in a prayer-like pose. The insect holds that pose until prey comes near. Then it shoots the forelegs out, impaling its victim on its spikes. The praying mantis eats its prey immediately. It mainly feeds on insects, but larger praying mantises hunt small birds, rodents, and reptiles.

Scorpion

Just arching its tail over its body is enough to turn away most predators that might hunt the scorpion. This arachnid stores venom in the stinger on the tip of its tail, ready to defend itself. It has two powerful, pinching front claws that help it capture and kill insects to eat. But the scorpion reserves the stinger and its poison to use on predators that want to eat it.

Defense Systems

Prey animals have learned ways to escape and defend themselves from attack without putting up a fight. Some animals can count on mimicry skills that make them look like a plant or blend into their environment—and remain unseen by predators. Some prey close themselves up in strong shells so that only the strongest predators can break inside. Other animals enlarge their appearance to bluff predators by seeming like a threat. To increase their chances of survival, some species have many, many offspring.

A small, spike-covered mammal called the hedgehog uses its prickly armor to protect itself from predators. The animal lives in wooded areas of Europe, Asia, and Africa, eating plants and hunting insects, frogs, and toads. If a predator finds it, the hedgehog rolls up to form a ball—with its soft belly and face inside and its sharp, hollow quills outside. Predators that try to bite or grab the animal receive painful pokes. Meanwhile, the hedgehog must use all of its strength to hold itself in the ball until the predator gives up.

Squid

Speed and great sight help the squid pursue fish, shrimp, and other prey in deep oceans and along coasts. But it needs a special skill to protect itself from sea creatures that would like to eat it.

So the squid releases dark ink that clouds the predator's vision. A second of darkness is enough time for the squid to race away from danger.

Sea Horse

The sea horse is a fish that is born with about 1,000 siblings—most of whom will be eaten by predators before they become adults. Because it has no defense against predators, the sea horse must rely on reproduction to improve its chances of surviving as a species. The eggs hatch from a pouch in the male sea horse's stomach.

Tree Frog

The tree frog doesn't have to put up a fight to fend off predators—the bright colors on its skin warns hunters that one bite of this amphibian could kill. Though the poison in the skin of a tree frog ranges from merely sickening to deadly, most predators don't take the chance!

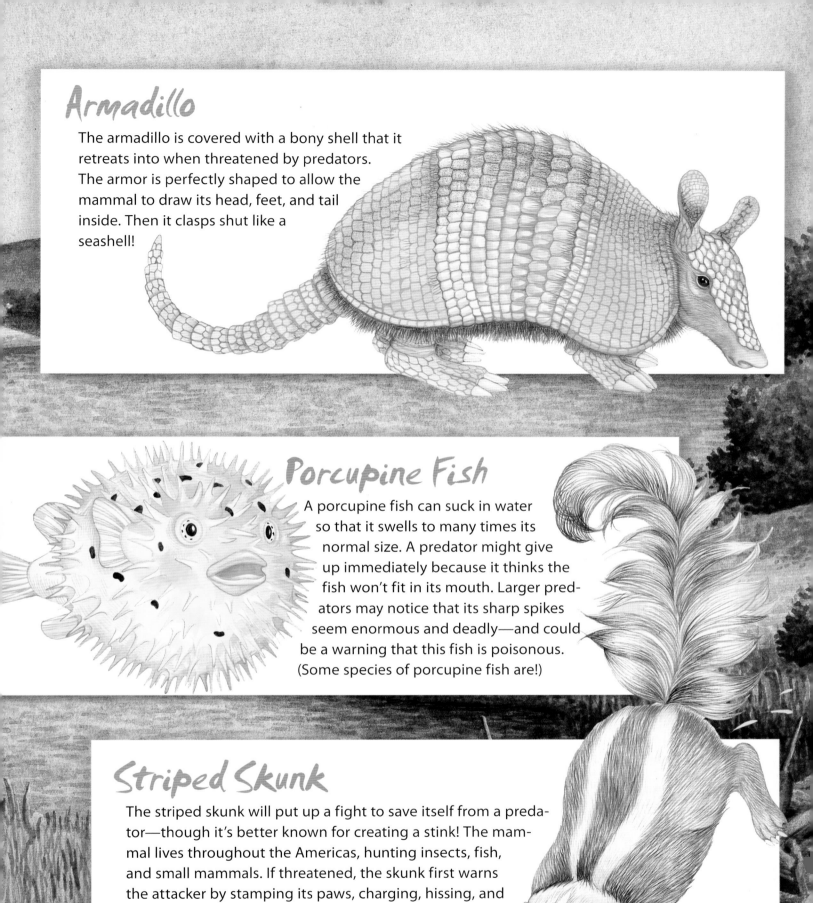

Armadillo

The armadillo is covered with a bony shell that it retreats into when threatened by predators. The armor is perfectly shaped to allow the mammal to draw its head, feet, and tail inside. Then it clasps shut like a seashell!

Porcupine Fish

A porcupine fish can suck in water so that it swells to many times its normal size. A predator might give up immediately because it thinks the fish won't fit in its mouth. Larger predators may notice that its sharp spikes seem enormous and deadly—and could be a warning that this fish is poisonous. (Some species of porcupine fish are!)

Striped Skunk

The striped skunk will put up a fight to save itself from a predator—though it's better known for creating a stink! The mammal lives throughout the Americas, hunting insects, fish, and small mammals. If threatened, the skunk first warns the attacker by stamping its paws, charging, hissing, and snarling. If that doesn't work, the skunk rears up and raises its tail. Most predators know what is next, and leave. If forced, the skunk points its tail at the predator and blasts a foul smelling liquid that can cause temporary blindness. Only crows, coyotes, and bobcats withstand the nauseating spray and eat the skunk.

The Food Chain

Scavengers are animals that eat carrion (dead animals). The parts that the scavengers eat provide them with energy. The parts they leave behind decay with the help of fungi and bacteria. The energy in those remains rejoins the food chain as nutrients in the soil.

Living things that share an environment pass energy along what's called a food chain. The sun powers the chain, and plants absorb the energy so they can grow. An animal eats a plant, taking in its energy. Then an even higher member of the food chain—a predator—eats that animal. Energy continues moving through the chain, as the predator becomes the prey of another predator or a scavenger. Tiny organisms called fungi and bacteria complete the chain: they feed on animal remains and return the energy to the soil in the form of nutrients.

Some carnivores are so powerful that they have no predators that can hunt them. Instead, these animals, like the lion, become food for scavengers after their deaths.

The sun is the ultimate source of energy that fuels the food chain.

Plants grow from the Earth, nourished by nutrients in the soil and by sunlight that powers the process of photosynthesis. Plants turn these resources into leaves, branches, and bark that animals can eat.

Herbivores are animals that eat plants. Some herbivores, like the zebra, become food for predators. This passes energy further along the food chain.

Carnivores feed on herbivores and, sometimes, other carnivores. The anteater is an example of a carnivore that is both predator and prey. The energy it gains from eating insects continues through the food chain to the animal that eats it.

Scavengers

Scavengers eat the carcasses that predators leave behind.

Hyena

The hyena's work begins where a predator's work ends. Its digestive system allows it to eat tough animal parts that even lions and tigers cannot.

The adult hyena has bone-breaking jaws that can crush skulls, ribs, and femurs with one bite. Inside the bones, the hyena finds and eats a substance called marrow that is full of nutrients.

Jackal

The jackal is a small canine that is both a predator and a scavenger. The jackal will hunt small mammals, birds, and reptiles, often chasing the prey until the victim is exhausted and unable to run further or defend itself. The jackal works in groups to take down larger prey, such as antelope. Scavenging a meal lets the jackal save energy.

Tasmanian Devil

The Tasmanian devil earns its fiendish reputation for its scary screeching, vicious snarling, and the foul odor it can emit. But the small marsupial needs all of these behaviors and skills to survive as a scavenger and to repel predators. It eats the carcasses of kangaroos, sheep, and cattle—bones, fur, and all!

Insects

Insects devour carcasses that other scavengers miss—and ones that are too small to make a meal for a vulture or a hyena. Some insects make a banquet out of a dead body, signaling for thousands of their kind to join the feast. Other insects lay their eggs in the carcass so that when the eggs hatch they'll have plenty to eat. The colonies of insect larvae develop among the remains, eating the carcass.

Condor

The condor is an enormous bird that scavenges its meals—sometimes eating so much that it can't fly until the food digests! It may overeat simply because it typically never leaves even a single bite of carcass to waste. The condor's size helps it frighten away competing scavengers. It has a wingspan of more than ten feet and can swoop down on carrion and easily carry it away to eat.

Vulture

Few scavenging animals can eat rotten or diseased flesh; the vulture is one that can. The bird lives in warmer climates on every continent except Antarctica, and the heat of its habitat helps it secure meals—and helps it fly. High temperatures speed the decay of carcasses so that they quickly become inedible to other animals. As ground-level air heated by the sun rises, it moves up in drafts that help the vulture take off and glide in circles to look for food.

Predators of the Past

Predators have been hunting prey for millions of years.

Saber-toothed Tiger

Scientists discovered that big cats used to have even bigger teeth. The saber-toothed tiger was a prehistoric predator that had 7-inch long fangs and weighed nearly 500 pounds. Its scientific name is smilodon, which means knife tooth. It went extinct about 11,000 years ago and its bones have been found in all areas of the world.

Huge Herbivores

Giant plant-eating dinosaurs may have been too large for predators to eat. The huge herbivores had small teeth and tiny claws that would not have offered much defense. They were also too slow and heavy to run, yet these species managed to survive for millions of years. Fossils reveal that some of these dinosaurs were covered in bony plates, which may have provided armor-like protection. Others had tails with spines that could have been used to strike at predators like clubs.

Flying Reptiles

During the age of dinosaurs, there were no birds. Instead, the skies were full of flying reptiles called pterosaurs. The large, winged lizards were both predators and prey. Some species of pterosaurs had hard beaks that they used to rip the flesh off small mammals. Beaks with thin teeth were ideal for catching fish.

Tyrannosaurus

One of the world's most famous predators is the tyrannosaurus. Its enormous mouth and foot-long teeth could grab up to 500 pounds in one bite. (If they had lived at the same time, a tyrannosaurus could have fit a smilodon in its mouth!) The tyrannosaurus was among the last and largest carnivorous dinosaurs and lived throughout North America about 65 million years ago. It stood nearly 21 feet tall, 40 feet long, and weighed as much as an elephant. No animals hunted this predator!

Glossary

Acceleration. An increase in the speed of movement.

Adapt. How an organism adjusts to its habitat to increase its chances of survival.

Aggressive. The way an animal behaves when it's about to attack another.

Algae. Organisms that grow in the water and feed by photosynthesis but are not plants.

Alpine. A high, cold area in the mountains, above where trees can grow.

Ambush. To hide and attack by surprise.

Amphibian. An animal that lives both in water and on land and has a backbone, cold blood, and moist, smooth skin.

Arachnid. An animal with four pairs of legs, a two-part body, no wings, and no backbone.

Beak. The horny exterior mouthpart of an animal.

Camouflage. Color, patterns, or other aspects of an animal appearance that help it blend in with its surroundings.

Carcass. The body of a dead animal.

Carnivore. An animal that eats other animals.

Claw. Pointed, curved, horn-like material at the end of an animal's toe.

Climate. An area's temperature, rainfall, snowfall, wind, and other weather conditions.

Colony. A group of the same kind of organism living together.

Crustacean. Animals with shells and segmented bodies and limbs that live in the water, such as shrimp, lobsters, and crabs.

Decay. To rot, to break down.

Energy. Exerting or using power. The ability to do work.

Environment. The conditions or surroundings that impact an organism's life.

Extinct. No longer alive. When no more animals of a certain species exist.

Fang. A long, sharply pointed tooth.

Fatal. Causing death.

Feline. A meat-eating mammal that is a member of the cat family.

Food chain. The relationships through which energy, in the form of food, is transferred between organisms in a community.

Fossil. The remains of an organism from long ago imprinted or preserved in rock or another hard material.

Fungi. Molds, mushrooms, and other organisms that use spores to reproduce.

Habitat. The area where an organism naturally lives.

Hatch. How young animals emerge from eggs.

Herbivore. An animal that eats plants.

Hibernate. When an animal's activity, body temperature, breathing, and heart rate slow to a sleep-like state to help it survive the cold weather and food shortages of winter.

Impale. To pierce or stab on a sharp point.

Larva. The first, immature stage of insect development, when the insect often appears worm-like and does not yet have wings. An insect in its larval stage.

Lethal. Causing death.

Mammal. Warm-blooded animals with young that drink milk produced by the mother.

Mate. The act of breeding between a male and a female animal that allows the female to become pregnant and give birth to or lay offspring.

Mimicry. When an organism looks like its surroundings or like another, more dangerous organism to protect itself from predators.

Mollusk. Animals, such as shellfish, squid, and octopi, that have soft, invertebrate bodies and hard shells. They usually live in water.

Natural selection. The process by which only organisms best suited to their environment pass on their genes and characteristics to future generations.

Nutrient. The substances in foods that provide energy.

Offspring. A new organism produced by reproduction.

Omnivore. An organism that eats both animals and plants.

Organ. A body part with a specific function.

Organism. A plant, animal, fungus, or other living thing.

Pack. A group of animals that live, travel, or hunt together.

Photosynthesis. The process through which plants turn light, water, and air into energy.

Predator. An animal that eats other animals.

Prehistoric. From a time long ago before people existed.

Prey. An animal that is hunted for food by another animal.

Puncture. To stab with a sharp point.

Reproduce. How organisms create another of their kind. Animals reproduce by mating and giving birth to young or laying eggs.

Ricochet. To strike a surface and bounce off.

Scavenger. An animal that feeds on dead animals it finds, rather than hunting and killing animals itself.

Sibling. A brother or sister; animals that have the same parents.

Skull. The bones and cartilage of the head.

Species. A kind or category of organism.

Suffocate. To die from lack of air.

Talon. A claw, especially the claw of a bird of prey.

Tentacle. A long, thin organ used to grasp or feel.

Trait. An inherited characteristic.

Tropical. The regions on either side of the Earth's equator where the climate is the hottest and most humid.

Upstream. In the opposite direction of water's flow.

Venom. A poisonous liquid that insects, snakes, and other organisms can inject by biting or stinging.

Wingspan. The distance from tip to tip of the wings when they are spread out.

Index